CONTENTS

POPULATION AND SETTLEMENT

People have settled all over the world, from the polar regions to the desert. We use the words 'population' and 'settlement' to talk about people and where they live.

POPULATION

Population means the number of people who live in an area. This might be the population of a city, a country or the whole planet.

With around 14 billion people, China has the largest population on Earth.

By 2030, the population of Delhi, India, could reach 39 million — making it the world's biggest city.

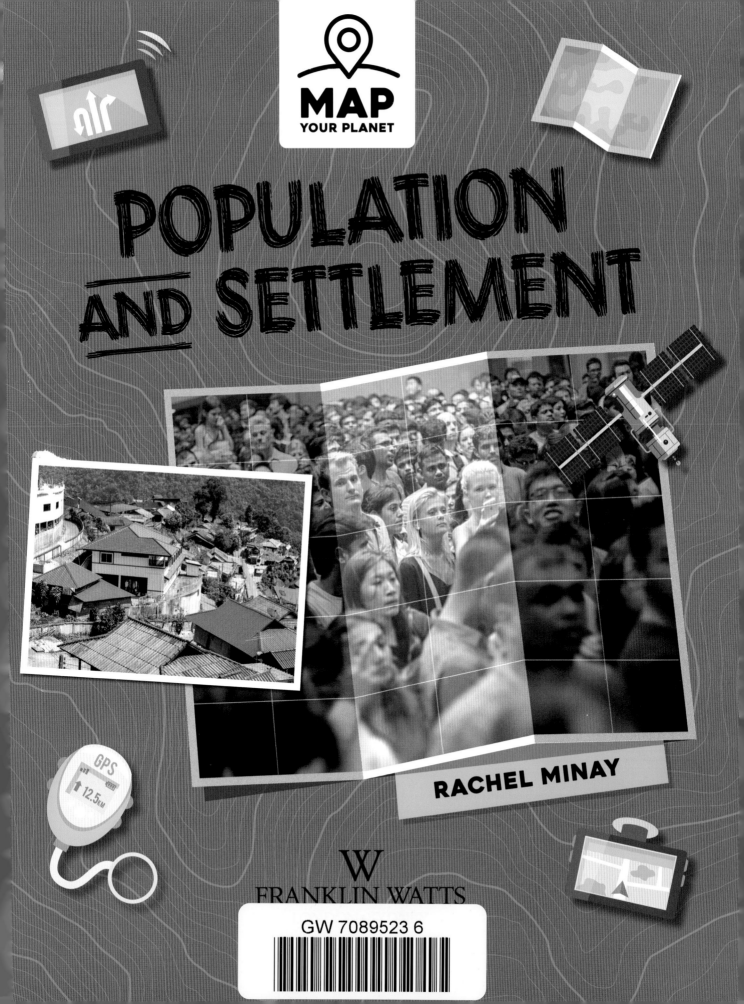

MAP
YOUR PLANET

POPULATION
AND SETTLEMENT

RACHEL MINAY

W
FRANKLIN WATTS

Franklin Watts

First published in Great Britain in 2021 by the Watts Publishing Group

Copyright © the Watts Publishing Group 2021

Produced for Franklin Watts by
White-Thomson Publishing Ltd
www.wtpub.co.uk

Editor: Rachel Minay
Series designer: Rocket Design (East Anglia) Ltd

HB ISBN 978 1 4451 7375 7
PB ISBN 978 1 4451 7376 4

The publisher would like to thank the following for permission to reproduce their pictures:
Alamy: Granger Historical Picture Archive 5(t), Matilde Gattoni/phocal Media 12(b), agefotostock 21(t), Lanmas 21(b);
Getty: ranplett 10(t); Library of Congress: Levick, Edwin 16(c), Detroit Photographic Co. 17(b); NASA (NASA Earth
Observatory mosaics by Joshua Stevens and Jesse Allen, using best pixel mosaics generated by Google Earth Engine
with Landsat data from the US Geological Survey): 28, 29; Shutterstock: Ok-product studio cover (inset), pzAxe cover
(main), testing 4(c), Don Mammoser 4(b), Orhan Cam 5(b), Kit Leong 6(b), Beata Tabak 7(t), donsimon 7(b), Pi-Lens 8(t),
kavram 8(b), MissRuby 9(t), Marzolino 9(b), Alphorom 11(t), MAHATHIR MOHD YASIN 13(b), Paolo Paradiso 14(c), Nicolas
Economou 15, ChameleonsEye 16(b), ActiveLines 18–19, SergiyN 19(t), Khanthachai C 19(b), Blue Planet Studio 22(c), Huw
Penson 23(c), IR Stone 24(c), r.nagy 24(b), Szymon Mucha 25(t), alice-photo 25(c), Josh Cornish 26(t), Dedan Photography
26(c), A. Mertens 27(t), Peter Stuckings 28(c), Sean Pavone 29(t).

Design elements by Shutterstock.

Map illustrations: Julian Baker: 8–9, 12, 13, 16–17, 20, 24–25.

Every effort has been made to clear copyright. Should there be any inadvertent omission,
please apply to the publisher for rectification.

The website addresses (URLs) included in this book were valid at the time of going to press.
However, it is possible that contents or addresses may have changed since the publication of this book.
No responsibility for any such changes can be accepted by either the author or the publisher.

All facts and statistics were correct at the time of press.

Printed in Dubai

Franklin Watts
An imprint of
Hachette Children's Group,
Part of the Watts Publishing Group
Carmelite House
50 Victoria Embankment
London EC4Y 0DZ

An Hachette UK Company
www.hachettechildrens.co.uk

SETTLEMENTS

A settlement is a place where people live and sometimes work. Settlements can be urban (cities or towns) or rural (in the countryside), and they can vary in size from a single home to a vast, sprawling megacity.

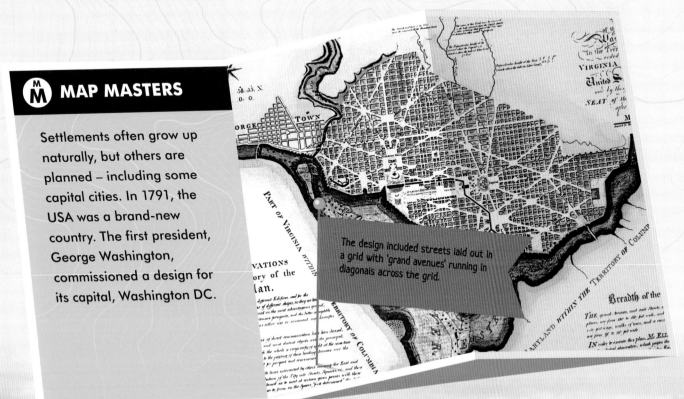

MAP MASTERS

Settlements often grow up naturally, but others are planned – including some capital cities. In 1791, the USA was a brand-new country. The first president, George Washington, commissioned a design for its capital, Washington DC.

The design included streets laid out in a grid with 'grand avenues' running in diagonals across the grid.

Over two centuries later, Washington still has the wide avenues and open spaces that were in the original plan.

DISTRIBUTION AND DENSITY

Countries differ in size in both land and population. Some stretch over a vast area but have few inhabitants, while some small islands are home to millions of people.

DISTRIBUTION

Population distribution means how people are spread out across an area. The distribution of the world's population is uneven – some places have many people and others very few.

DENSITY

Population density is the number of people living in a specific area, usually 1 square km. It varies across countries, but also within countries. The most densely populated areas within a country tend to be in cities and along coasts.

Some places, such as small countries like Monaco, are densely populated.

Three-quarters of Greenland is under ice, so this is a sparsely populated country with all the main settlements on the ice-free coast

REASONS TO SETTLE

People are more likely to settle in a place with a mild climate, flat land and fertile soil, and which is near to resources, such as water. Other reasons might include the number of jobs available and good transport links. People are less likely to settle where it is hard to live and work, for example where the climate is extremely hot or cold, where the soil is difficult to farm, or where there are few jobs.

Manila is the capital of the Philippines. With an average of over 46,000 people living in 1 square km, it is the world's most densely populated city.

MAPPING GLOBAL POPULATION

This map shows how the world's population is spread out. The darker the green, the more densely populated the area. How does where you live compare with the rest of the world?

The world's average population density is around 60 people per square km.

1 CANADA

Canada is the world's second biggest country (after Russia) but has one of the lowest population densities — just 4 people per square km.

Much of this cold country is forested and mountainous.

2 NETHERLANDS

The Netherlands is a flat, fertile land with a mild climate. With 511 people per square km, it has one of the highest population densities in Europe.

The vast Namib Desert runs the length of Namibia's coast.

3 NAMIBIA

Namibia is Africa's least densely populated country — just 3 people per square km.

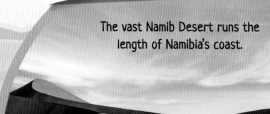

④ AUSTRALIA

Around 25 million people live in Australia, but its density of just 3 people per square km is one of the world's lowest. Most people live in cities on the east coast.

⑤ BANGLADESH

Bangladesh is a small country with a big population. It has a high density of 1,240 people per square km.

In population tables, Bangladesh is 8th in the world; but it sits in 92nd place for land area.

Ⓜ MAP MASTERS

Paul Vidal de la Blache was a French geographer who was interested in how people interact with their environment. He made this population density map around 125 years ago. How does it compare with the modern map on this page?

POPULATION GROWTH

The world population didn't reach 1 billion until 1804, but there has been a population explosion over the last hundred years, taking the world population total to near 9 billion. However, it is now growing more slowly, and could even peak within the next 50 years.

GROWTH

The population of a country increases when there are more births than deaths. Better healthcare means more children live into adulthood and are able to reproduce. The birth rate is also affected by things such as access to and education about contraception, while the death rate can be affected by things such as war and disease.

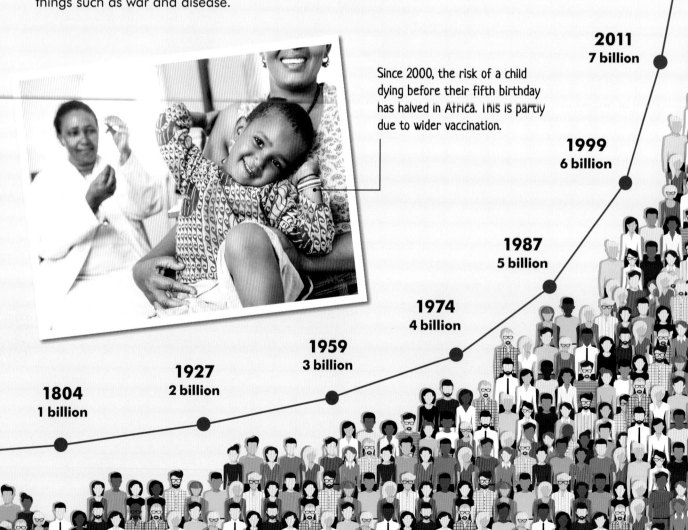

Since 2000, the risk of a child dying before their fifth birthday has halved in Africa. This is partly due to wider vaccination.

2064
9.7 billion?

2011
7 billion

1999
6 billion

1987
5 billion

1974
4 billion

1959
3 billion

1927
2 billion

1804
1 billion

INCOME

Population growth is linked to how much people earn, with low-income countries tending to have high birth and death rates. Currently, most of the fastest-growing countries in the world are in Africa, where birth rates are high and people are living longer. Countries growing fast brings huge opportunities, but also presents problems.

Nearly half of the population of the Democratic Republic of the Congo (DRC) are 14 or under. This means a potentially large future workforce, but the country faces many challenges. The DRC is rich in resources, but years of conflict and corruption mean most people live in extreme poverty.

FACT

Fertility rates are now falling in many countries. Recent research says the world population could peak at 9.7 billion around 2064.

OVERPOPULATION?

Are there too many people in the world? More people means greater pressure on food, water and other precious resources, as well as on space for housing. Larger numbers of people also create more waste and pollution. We should all use resources more carefully to live in a more sustainable way.

More people means more pollution, leading to global warming and climate change.

MAPPING
NIGER AND JAPAN

Countries can be very different in both population and settlement. This includes population structure – how many people of different ages there are.

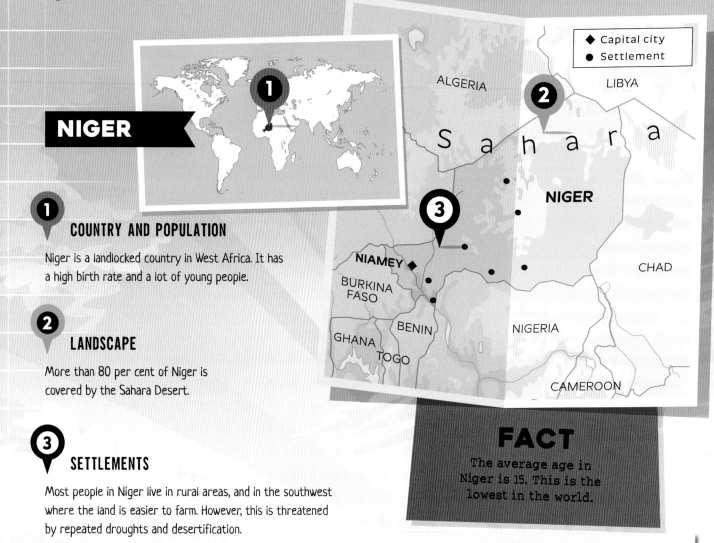

NIGER

Capital city
Settlement

ALGERIA
LIBYA
Sahara
NIGER
NIAMEY
BURKINA FASO
BENIN
GHANA
TOGO
NIGERIA
CHAD
CAMEROON

1. COUNTRY AND POPULATION

Niger is a landlocked country in West Africa. It has a high birth rate and a lot of young people.

2. LANDSCAPE

More than 80 per cent of Niger is covered by the Sahara Desert.

3. SETTLEMENTS

Most people in Niger live in rural areas, and in the southwest where the land is easier to farm. However, this is threatened by repeated droughts and desertification.

FACT

The average age in Niger is 15. This is the lowest in the world.

Women in Niger have an average of seven children. This is the highest fertility rate in the world.

CHALLENGES

Niger is a low-income country and it has very low literacy rates, particularly among women and girls. The country will need jobs in order to feed, educate and provide healthcare for its fast-growing population.

JAPAN

① COUNTRY AND POPULATION

Japan is an island country in East Asia. It has a low birth rate and an ageing population.

② LANDSCAPE

Much of Japan is mountainous and forested.

③ SETTLEMENTS

Japan has a very urban population. Most of its 126 million people live in densely packed cities around the coasts.

Excellent healthcare and a healthy diet mean Japan has one of the world's highest life expectancies — around 83 years.

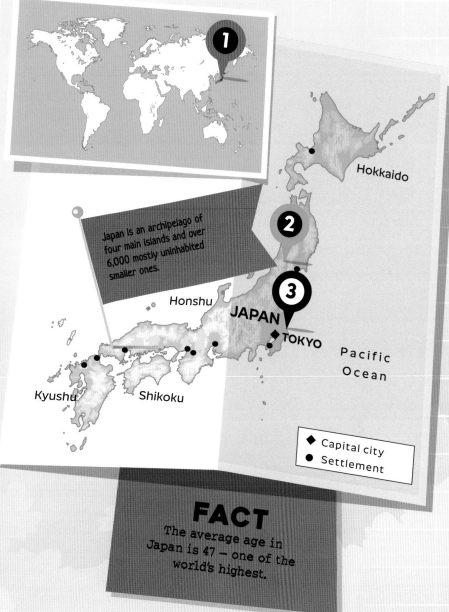

Japan is an archipelago of four main islands and over 6,000 mostly uninhabited smaller ones.

Hokkaido

Honshu

JAPAN

◆ TOKYO

Kyushu

Shikoku

Pacific Ocean

◆ Capital city
● Settlement

FACT
The average age in Japan is 47 — one of the world's highest.

CHALLENGES

Japan is one of the world's largest economies, but its birth rate has become so low that the population is shrinking. This could be a real problem if there are not enough adults in the future to support industry and care for the large elderly population.

MIGRATION

Migration is when people move and settle in a new location permanently. This can be between countries or within them, for example moving from the countryside to find work in a city.

ON THE MOVE

Emigration is when people move out of a country. Immigration is when people move into another one. Sometimes people choose to move voluntarily; sometimes they are forced to move, for example due to war or natural disaster. The reasons people want to move are often called push and pull factors.

Immigration can bring a more diverse and rich culture.

PUSH FACTORS

Push factors are things that make people want to move **away** from the area or country they live in. For example:

- **few jobs**
- **few services**
- **poor transport links**
- **conflict or war**
- **natural disasters, such as a volcanic eruption**
- **famine.**

PULL FACTORS

Pull factors are things that make people want to move **to** the new place. For example:

- **job opportunities**
- **access to services, such as better healthcare**
- **better transport links**
- **hope for a better life**
- **to be near family.**

People fleeing conflict often undertake extremely dangerous journeys in their hope for a new life. These Syrian refugees are travelling by boat to Greece.

FACT

In 2019, the number of international migrants reached 272 million.

About half of all international migrants live in just ten countries.

USA 51 million	Germany 13 million	Saudi Arabia 13 million	Russia 12 million	UK 10 million	UAE 9 million	France 8 million	Canada 8 million	Australia 8 million	Italy 6 million

MAPPING
US IMMIGRATION

The ancestors of Native Americans moved to North America from Asia around 20,000 years ago. Europeans began settling from around 1600. So many people have made the USA their home since then, the country is sometimes called a 'nation of immigrants'.

At times in its history, the USA has encouraged immigration; at other times, it has passed acts to limit it.

ASIA

Pacific Ocean

OCEANIA

4

① EUROPE

Europeans settled in America from the seventeenth century. Some were fleeing religious persecution, while others saw the country as a land of opportunity. Emigration from Europe boomed over the following centuries.

Between 1880 and 1920 more than 20 million immigrants arrived from Europe.

② NEW YORK AND ELLIS ISLAND

New York was known as the 'Golden Door' — 70 per cent of all immigrants entered here. In 1892 a centre to process them opened on Ellis Island.

Ellis Island ———

FACT

In 1907 alone, 1.3 million people came through Ellis Island.

③ AFRICA

Although many people chose to move to America in hope of a better life, others came against their will. Between the seventeenth and nineteenth centuries, around 500,000 Africans were brought and sold into slavery.

④ CHINA

Thousands emigrated from China in the nineteenth century, usually via the US west coast. Initially attracted by the California gold rush, Chinese immigrants later worked on the railroads and as miners. Many suffered discrimination, and in 1882 an act was passed to ban them from entering the country.

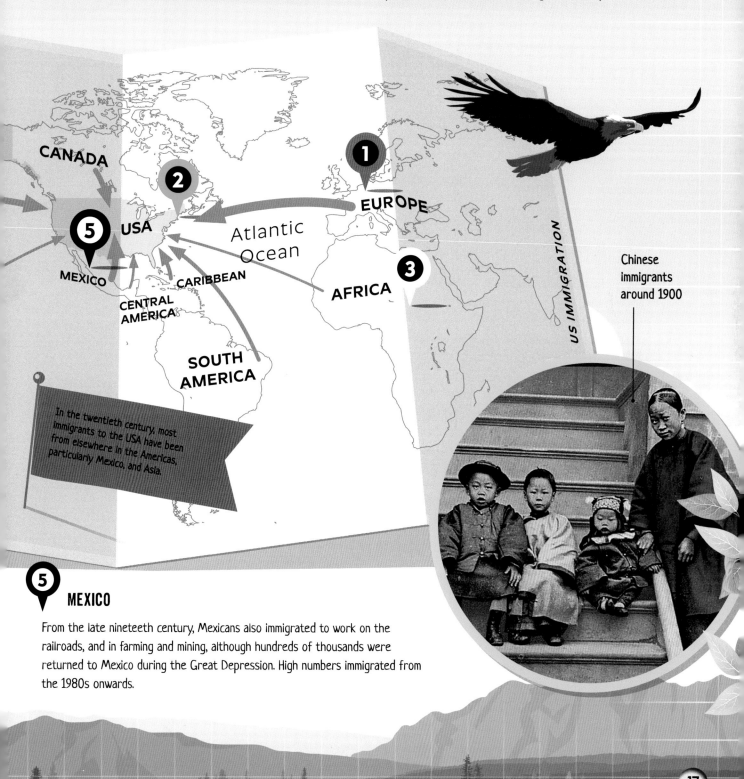

CANADA

② USA

⑤

MEXICO

CENTRAL AMERICA

CARIBBEAN

Atlantic Ocean

① EUROPE

③ AFRICA

SOUTH AMERICA

US IMMIGRATION

In the twentieth century, most immigrants to the USA have been from elsewhere in the Americas, particularly Mexico, and Asia.

Chinese immigrants around 1900

⑤ MEXICO

From the late nineteenth century, Mexicans also immigrated to work on the railroads, and in farming and mining, although hundreds of thousands were returned to Mexico during the Great Depression. High numbers immigrated from the 1980s onwards.

EARLY SETTLEMENTS

Early settlements usually grew up in places that were safe from attack or flood, with flat, fertile land, and close to water and other resources. Things like transport links to other settlements would help them to grow.

SITE

A site is the land a settlement is built on. Early settlers looked for sites with:

- flat land, so building was easier

- building materials, such as wood and stone

- a water supply

- dry land that wouldn't flood

- natural defence, for example a hilltop or bend in a river

- fertile soil

- shelter to protect from bad weather.

SITUATION

Situation is how close the settlement is to features in the environment and other places. Situation factors that would help an early settlement to grow include being:

- a route centre (like a crossroads)

- at a low point on a river, where it was easy to ford or cross

- a port

- a gap town (between two hills)

- close to minerals that could be exported.

Which features of this site make it good for a settlement? What would make it better?

Barcelona in Spain grew from an early settlement that had a water supply, hills for shelter and defence, and fertile flat land. It has been a port for 2,000 years.

Bhutan is a landlocked country in the Himalayas. Steep ground and a harsh climate mean building, farming and travelling would have been very challenging for early settlers.

MAPPING
TENOCHTITLAN

In 1325, the Mexica people were looking for a place to settle. Legend says they were looking for a sign – an eagle with a snake in its beak, perched on a cactus. When they saw it on an island in the middle of a lake, they built a mighty Aztec city – Tenochtitlan.

LAKE TEXCOCO

The lake was in the middle of a wooded valley surrounded by hills. There were plenty of birds and fish the Mexica could catch for food.

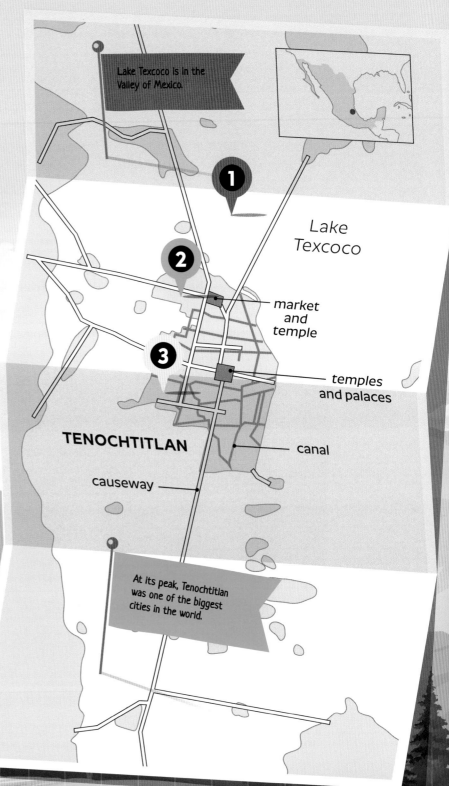

Lake Texcoco is in the Valley of Mexico.

Lake Texcoco

market and temple

temples and palaces

canal

TENOCHTITLAN

causeway

At its peak, Tenochtitlan was one of the biggest cities in the world.

② ISLAND LIFE

A swampy island might seem an odd place to build a capital city, but the water made a natural defence. The Mexica built causeways to reach the mainland and bridges that could be removed in case of attack. They grew crops in the lake, in raised beds that looked like floating gardens.

③ CITY PLANNING

The city was carefully planned and laid out in a symmetrical grid of four zones with great temples and palaces in the centre. Canals were built to make moving around the city easier.

This painting by Mexican artist Diego Rivera imagines what life was like in Tenochtitlan.

Ⓜ MAP MASTERS

This map from 1524 shows the buildings, canals and causeways of this incredible island city. Just three years before the map was made, the Spanish conquered the Aztec Empire and destroyed Tenochtitlan. Mexico City grew up in its place.

SETTLEMENT TYPES AND PATTERNS

Settlements come in different shapes and sizes. Bigger settlements have more things like shops, schools and leisure facilities.

TYPES OF SETTLEMENT

There are different ways to define settlements, but they can roughly be described in terms of population size:

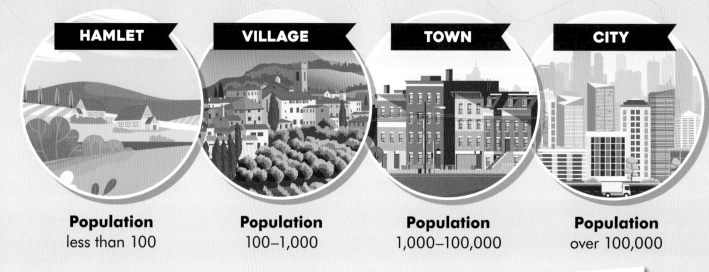

HAMLET

Population
less than 100

VILLAGE

Population
100–1,000

TOWN

Population
1,000–100,000

CITY

Population
over 100,000

A city of over 10 million people is often called a megacity. Tokyo, Japan, is the world's biggest megacity.

How many people live in Tokyo? Turn to page 27 to find out.

PATTERNS

Urban settlements often follow a pattern, with different zones spreading out from the centre.

SUBURBS INNER CITY CBD

- The central business district (CBD) is the commercial or financial centre of the city.

- Historically, the inner city was where factories and the houses of factory workers were. These areas often became run down, but are increasingly being regenerated.

- Suburban houses are usually bigger and have more outside space than typical inner-city houses. Good transport links means they are often home to commuters who work in the city.

St Davids in Wales is a city, but has a population of only around 1,500 people.

WHAT MAKES A VILLAGE OR A CITY?

What is seen as a village in one country might be considered a hamlet or a town in other parts of the world. Cities are nearly always large, but in the UK a city is decided by the monarch and traditionally was a settlement with a cathedral.

MAPPING LONDON

London was founded by the Romans in 43 CE. By the seventeenth century, the population was bursting the original city walls and it started to spread. Today, it is home to around 9 million people.

1 CITY OF LONDON

The 'City' or 'Square Mile' is the historic centre and also the main CBD or financial district. This tiny area of modern-day London was the whole of the city from Roman times to the Middle Ages.

City of London ⎯⎯⎯⎯⎯⎯⎯

London is the capital of England and the UK.

2 CANARY WHARF

London's second CBD is Canary Wharf. It is on a peninsula in the Thames in the East of London.

3 INNER LONDON

London really started to expand in the Victorian era, due in large part to the railways.

Inner London is now one of the wealthiest areas in Europe, but there is also widespread poverty.

OUTER LONDON

In the first half of the twentieth century, many people moved from crowded Inner London to the greener suburbs.

Croydon is a large town in Outer London.

Map legend:
- City of London
- Inner London
- Outer London
- Green Belt

River Thames

GREEN BELT

Some UK cities, including London, are surrounded by a green belt — a ring of countryside that planners should not build on. Green belts are designed to stop urban sprawl and to provide outdoor space for people living in the city.

FACT

By 1840 London was the biggest city in the world.

MAP MASTERS

The London Underground opened in 1863. Its unusual map doesn't show the position of stations as they really are, but simply how they relate and connect to each other. The idea is that the people using the map are underground, so physical locations don't matter — as long as they reach their destination!

CHANGING SETTLEMENTS

As the previous pages on London clearly show, settlements can change a lot over time.

INNER-CITY PROBLEMS

Sudden urban growth can lead to problems in inner cities, including overcrowding, traffic congestion, air pollution, low-quality housing and a lack of green space. This means people often escape city centres to start a new life in the suburbs. Over time, growing suburbs can result in urban sprawl if there is no protection to stop building.

In the early twentieth century, Detroit was a US industrial powerhouse thanks to the car industry. First the factories and then people moved to the suburbs, leaving an inner-city 'ghost town', with thousands of abandoned buildings.

In recent years, Detroit has worked hard to revitalise the city, building new homes and improving things such as public transport, streetlights and parks.

CITY

SUBURBS

CITY LIVING

As industry in city centres has declined, this pattern of moving outwards has changed in many cities. Old buildings can be demolished and replaced with new housing or offices – this is called regeneration. City centres are still popular places to live because they are close to shops and other amenities, have good transport links and often have close-knit communities. In recent years, there has been a trend of people moving back into cities – this is called re-urbanisation.

Converting inner-city buildings into high-quality housing can lead to gentrification. This is when development causes prices to be pushed up, forcing local people out of an area.

FACT

It is predicted that more than two-thirds of the world population will live in urban areas by 2050.

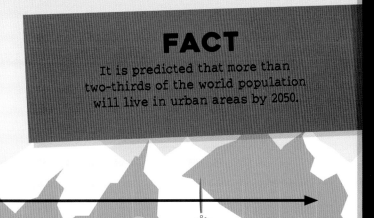

TOP TEN

These are the 10 biggest cities by urban area (population in millions).

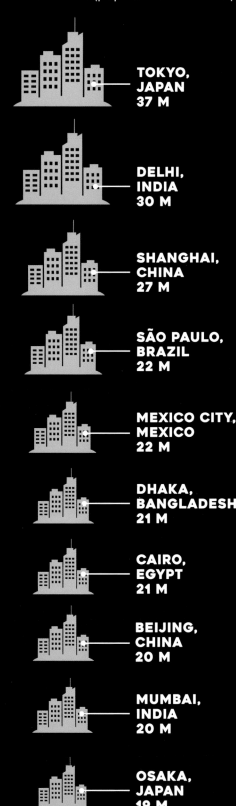

TOKYO, JAPAN
37 M

DELHI, INDIA
30 M

SHANGHAI, CHINA
27 M

SÃO PAULO, BRAZIL
22 M

MEXICO CITY, MEXICO
22 M

DHAKA, BANGLADESH
21 M

CAIRO, EGYPT
21 M

BEIJING, CHINA
20 M

MUMBAI, INDIA
20 M

OSAKA, JAPAN
19 M

MAPPING
SHANGHAI

In recent years, Shanghai in China has been one of the world's fastest developing cities.

① TRADE AND FINANCE

Shanghai's position on an estuary of the Yangtze River helped it grow from a small village to an important port. Big investment and redevelopment in the 1990s mean it is now the world's largest container port and a leader in trade and finance.

MAP MASTERS

Satellite technology can map the Earth in increasing detail. The NASA maps on this page are 'best pixel mosaics', which means they are made from the best parts of many satellite images. This avoids any clouds or haze to show Shanghai's phenomenal growth.

Shanghai built a new financial district in the 1990s.

These two satellite maps show Shanghai from two different time periods.

SHANGHAI 1988

Wuxi

③

Yangtze River

①

②

Lake Tai

Suzhou

Shanghai

FACT
In 1960, 110 million Chinese people lived in cities; by 2015, this figure had leapt to 760 million.

② CITY CENTRE

Look at the size of Shanghai in the first map. There are also settlements at Wuxi and Suzhou, but most of the map is farmland. By 2017, the land is filled with houses, factories, shops and roads.

Between 1982 and 2016, the population of Shanghai doubled from 12 to 24 million.

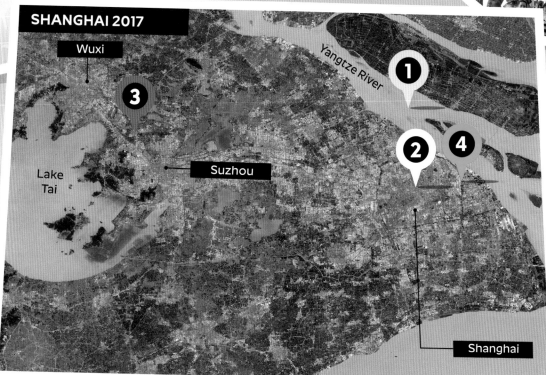

SHANGHAI 2017

Wuxi

③

Yangtze River

①

Lake Tai

② ④

Suzhou

Shanghai

③ URBAN SPRAWL

In the first map, the cities of Suzhou and Wuxi are clearly separate. By 2017, they have merged with Shanghai to form a huge megalopolis.

④ GREEN SPACE

It is clear how much open space has been lost by 2017, but you might be able to spot a green line around the city centre. This is made up of parks and forest and was designed to give Shanghai's city-dwellers some access to green space.

GLOSSARY

archipelago a large group of islands

causeway a raised track across low ground or water

climate change the rising temperature of the Earth's surface and its effects, such as melting ice caps and more extreme weather

contraception using birth control to prevent pregnancy

desertification when land permanently loses its fertility, so things that grew in the past will no longer grow

discrimination when someone is treated differently or unfairly because of something like their race, sex or religion

emigration when people move out of a country

estuary the mouth of a river where it meets the sea

fertility rate the average number of children born to a woman over a lifetime

global warming the rising temperature of the Earth's surface; it is caused by very high levels of carbon dioxide and other greenhouse gases in the atmosphere

Great Depression a major financial crisis of the 1930s that started in the USA

immigration when people move into a new country

income how much people earn

life expectancy the average age someone in a particular country might be expected to live to

literacy rate the proportion of the population able to read and write

Mexica people of the Valley of Mexico who became the rulers of the Aztec Empire

migration when people move and settle in a new place permanently

peninsula a piece of land almost surrounded by water

persecution when someone is treated badly because of their beliefs

pollution the act of damaging the natural world with harmful substances

refugee someone who has had to leave their home because of something such as war or famine

regeneration when an area is upgraded, improving its buildings and its economy

sustainable describes something that can continue for a long time because it does not harm the environment

urban sprawl when a city spreads into the area around it without planning

FURTHER INFORMATION

Books

Settlements (Fact Planet) by Izzi Howell (Franklin Watts, 2020)

Overpopulation (Ecographics) by Izzi Howell (Franklin Watts, 2020)

Population and Settlement (Geographics) by Izzi Howell (Franklin Watts, 2017)

Websites

www.populationpyramid.net
Population structure can be shown in a graph called a population pyramid. You can compare pyramids for different countries here. Check out your own country – what does the population structure look like?

www.3dgeography.co.uk/settlement-geography
Find out more about settlements and follow the links to watch videos or make 3D models.

populationmatters.org/the-facts/the-numbers
Discover more population facts at this site by UK-based charity Population Matters.

INDEX